SYDNEY

Yvonne Shafir

Sydney at the Turn of the Millennium

From her lowly beginnings as a convict settlement in the late eighteenth century, Sydney is soaring into the new millennium as one of the world's most stylish and cosmopolitan cities. No longer bound by her geographical isolation, the premier state's (as New South Wales is called) premier city is host to the Olympic Games in the year 2000, and is one of the hottest international travel destinations. Yet Sydneysiders, who modestly proclaim their home as "the best address on earth" have long appreciated the city's infinite pleasures: the sun and surf; the café culture and fine cuisine; the cultural treasures – both colonial and contemporary; the multicultural *mélange*, and the decadent nightlife.

From a visual perspective, with the breathtaking scenery of its harbour, cliffs and beaches, and ample parks and gardens, Sydney is the most picturesque (dare we say 'operatic') of urban environments. The city itself however is not an exemplary model of urban planning, with many streets simply tracing the colonial bullock paths upwards from the harbour. As a result, a haphazard group of neighbourhoods with distinct personalities – including Chinatown, Darlinghurst, the Rocks, Kings Cross – are wedged together around the city centre albeit interspersed with large expanses of greenery, such as the Domain and vast concrete pedestrian malls like those at Darling Harbour. Fine examples of Georgian and Victorian architecture abound, from the great bastions of civic power in the central business district and Macquarie Street to the famed terrace houses of Paddington. Beyond the city centre lie chic residential neighbourhoods and the natural wonders of sea and sand – most notably Bondi and Manly beaches – which are as much a part of Sydney's iconography as the Harbour Bridge and the Opera House.

The Central Business District

From a distance, the imposing skyline of Sydney's central business district, known as CBD, would seem to confirm the city's claim (hotly disputed by its historical rival, Melbourne!) of being the business capital of Australia. The claim to commercial precedence is not however reflected in the district's girth, a relatively small area bounded by Circular Quay to the north, Chinatown to the south, Darling Harbour to the west, and on the eastern periphery by the green expanse extending from the Domain to Hyde Park.

1. Sydney CBD
2. Archibald Fountain (1932) in Hyde Park by French sculptor F. Sicard features motifs from Greek mythology.
3. Sydney's famed sunlight creates gorgeous reflections in the glass façades of city buildings
4. A view of Sydney Cove

3

Hyde Park, named after its London predecessor, originally marked the outskirts of the township. Today it forms a leisurely breach in the city's commercial tide, with its handsome public art and luxurious lawns.

Alongside is the city's central hub, a compact grid dissected horizontally by pedestrian malls and vertically overshadowed by modern towers such as the elegant Chifley Square. From close-by, the citadel of steel and glass is tempered by buildings which, while smaller in scale, emanate a poetic grandeur.

On streets whose names reflect the early Australian obsession with its British forbears – Clarence, Kent, Pitt, George and Elizabeth – rise the architectural fantasies of the Victorian Age. Eclectically borrowing from earlier periods, Victorian architects fashioned a series of monumental buildings in sandstone quarried from nearby Pyrmont. Colonnaded edifices in the Classical Revival style soberly reside as backdrops to the bustle of lunchtime crowds of office-workers, while Romanesque façades beam capriciously at shoppers segueing from speciality shops to departments stores.

5

6

5. View of the city from Bennelong Point, site of the Sydney Opera House
6. Hyde Park
7. Contemporary Sydney architecture
8. A view of the city (photo shot from the Opera House)

George Street, whose kingly sway through the length of the CBD resembles a grand New York avenue, is home to many fine examples of Victoriana. At the southern end near Sydney Square glower the lion-heads on the ornate façade of the Town Hall, Sydney's most elaborate building. At a few steps southwards on Sydney Square, in imitation of York Minster, hover the twin peaks of Sydney's oldest Gothic Revival cathedral, St. Andrews. On the eastern edge of Hyde Park is the precious Great Synagogue, home to Sydney's longest established Jewish congregation and perhaps the finest work of Sydney Hospital architect, Thomas Rowe. A short stroll away across the green lawns to the park's western edge is St. Mary's, the Gothic Revival style cathedral serving Sydney's Catholic population.

9

10

9. Contemporary Sydney
   architecture
10. Detail of dome in Town Hall
11. The elaborate Queen
    Victoria Building
12. Café in Queen Victoria
    Building

13

14

13. The Central Business
    District is linked to the
    North Shore by the
    Sydney Harbour Bridge
    completed in 1932.
14. Centrepoint Tower
15. Towers

15

Heading northwards along George Street and occupying an entire city block is what Pierre Cardin has called "the most beautiful shopping centre in the world". The Queen Victoria building, an ornamental Romanesque structure built to resemble a Byzantine palace closed its doors as a city produce market at the end of World War One and reopened in 1986 as a shopping gallery housing up-scale boutiques and cafés. Opposite the QVB, resurrected in the basement of the Hilton hotel, dwells the decadent Italian Renaissance-style Marble Bar. Initially part of George Adam's Tattersall's hotel of 1893, the bar with its stained glass panels and rich woodwork – the site of many a secret Victorian tryst – was dismantled and lovingly reassembled when the original hotel was torn down.

17

18

16. Inside the sumptuous Queen Victoria Building. Suspended from the ceiling and weighing in at one ton is the Royal Clock (1982) designed by Neil Glasser.
17. Painted façade in the CBD
18. View of the MLC Centre at Martin Place from the Centre Point

19

Another fancifully ostentatious Sydney institution is located around the corner on Market Street. The State Theatre, originally a movie palace and once hailed as "the Empire's greatest theatre" opened in 1929. It is an extravagant example of Cinema Baroque style, with a mosaic tiled Gothic foyer studded with decoratively carved marble columns and statues.

20

19. Façade at Bulletin Place
20. Flower
21. Archibald Fountain in Hyde Park

21

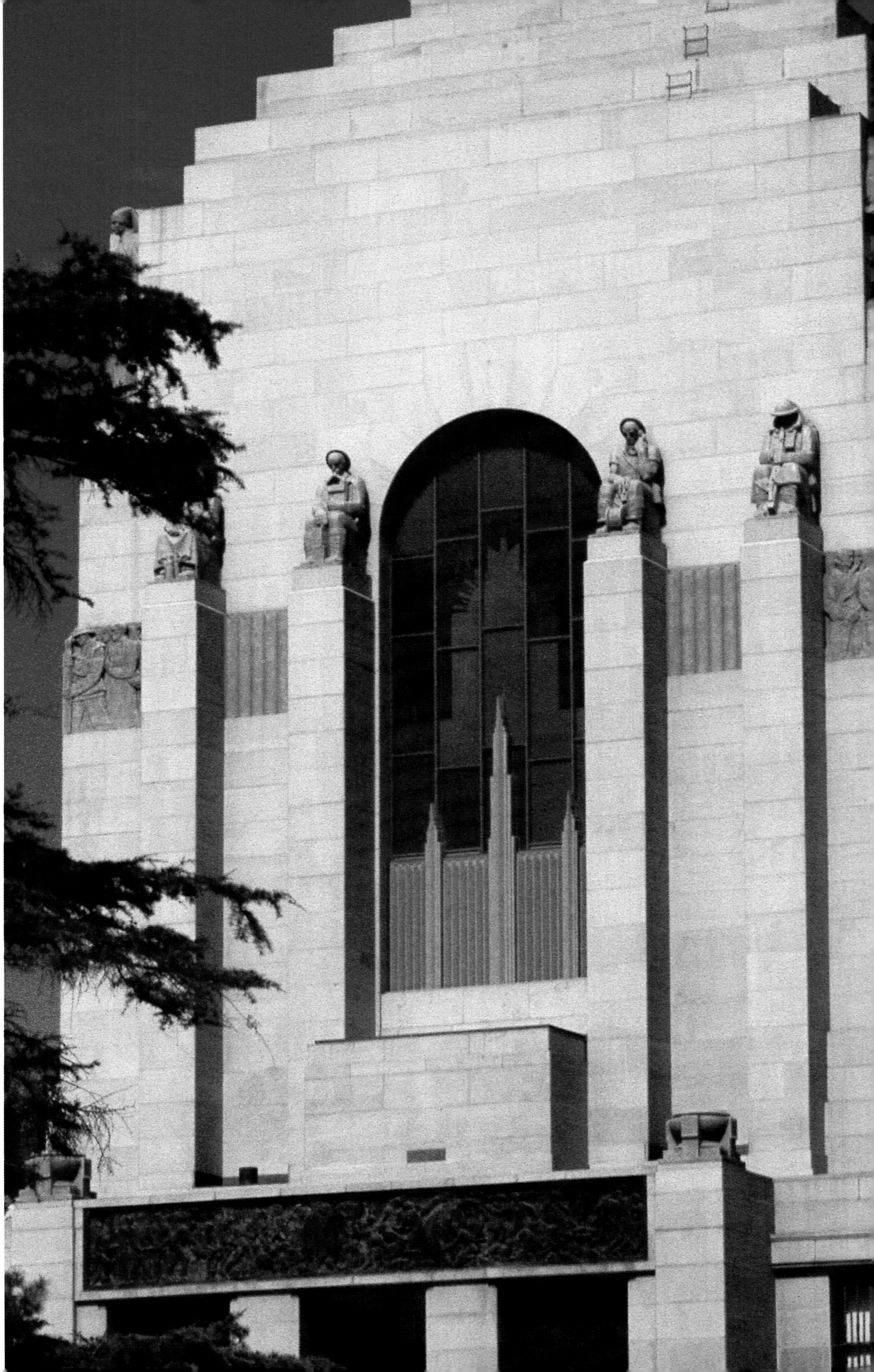

Steps away from the State Theatre on Market Street atop the 1970s Centrepoint shopping centre looms a landmark of another age. From the giant turret of the Sydney Tower, the tallest building in the Southern Hemisphere, more than a million visitors each year are afforded panoramic views over the city and beyond to the Blue Mountains.

Victorian Sydney was a city of grand shopping arcades and The Strand, which joins George and Pitt Streets, was its most majestic. Designed by John Spencer in 1892, this airy arcade is lit with natural Sydney sunlight from its glass roof, and by the incandescence of chandeliers that bedeck its ceilings like strands of jewels.

Just north of The Strand, bounded by George and Macquarie Streets is the open-air mall, Martin Place. The plaza is imposingly lined with the sandstone banks and offices that are ciphers of the city's late nineteenth-century economic boom. At the George Street end is the Cenotaph war memorial by Bertram MacKennal – gathering point of the Anzac Day parade in April and the site of Sydney's glittering summertime Christmas tree. On the southern side of the Cenotaph is the monolithic, Renaissance style General Post Office considered to be the finest work of James Barnet, whose Classical Revival Lands Department Building lies further north on Bridge Street.

23   24

22. Anzac Memorial in Hyde Park
23. View of the 305m high Centrepoint down
    on the swimming pool of a hotel
24. Quarterhouse

Perhaps the best perspective of the city is to be gleaned from the nearby Museum of Sydney. Here on the site of the first Government House, Sydney's tumultuous history from 1788 to 1850 is recalled, while an entire floor is devoted to an exhibition about the Eora people who lived in the Sydney basin prior to the arrival of the British.

25. Hyde Park and the Sydney Tower
26. The city skyline at dusk

25

The Domain

To the east of the CBD's sandstone public buildings, the crenellated wall of high-rises and their progeny of concrete wind-tunnels unfurls an almost uninterrupted carpet of greenery leading down from the Domain, through the Royal Botanical Gardens to Hyde Park. This verdant oasis owes its legacy to Governor Lachlan Macquarie who sought to replicate the genteel life of English society – with its love of parks and gardens – within the fledgling colony. Thanks to the conservation efforts of the late twentieth century in restoring many of the buildings along Macquarie Street, it takes little to conjur up an image of Sydney's refined Victorian past, notwithstanding periodic glimpses of the Opera House!

Tree-lined Macquarie Street which runs from the Opera House southwards to Hyde Park, dividing the city centre from the natural wonderland to the east, resembles a European boulevard in its grand sweep. Saturated with history and dripping with old money, it is laced on the northern end by the elegant nineteenth-century terrace homes which once housed Sydney's urban gentry.

A breath of 1900 awaits just steps away in a strip of medical practices, reminiscent of London's Harley Street, that continue until this day. Dating from the same period is the winged portico of the Mitchell Library, the original section of the subsequently enlarged State Library of New South Wales which offers a voluminous wealth of archival, research and exhibition facilities.

27. The columned façade of the Art Gallery of New South Wales
28. Little flowers

Alongside the Library unfolds a regal succession of Victorian and Georgian public buildings which once housed the Rum Hospital (so-called because its builders were paid in liquor). Today in the former northern wing – an ornate corrugated-iron building – sits Parliament House, whose legislative assembly is familiarly referred to as the "bear-pit" due to its members' notorious approach to debate. The Sydney Hospital, an august assemblage of Classical Revival buildings is situated within the earlier hospital's central section. In the former southern wing is the sprawling colonial Sydney Mint Museum whose exhibits commemorate the period in which the building served as the first Royal Mint outside of London.

The imposing size of these civic edifices looms large in the imagination when one considers how small the city was at the time they were built. While convicts supplied the man-power for their construction, it was a convicted forger, Francis Greenway, who was the colonial architect responsible for designing the elegant Georgian Hyde Park Barracks nearby. Built between 1817 and 1819 to house the colony's 800 convicts, the building praised by Governor Macquarie as "airy" and "spacious" has been an orphanage, a women's asylum and legal offices until it was refurbished in 1900 and reopened as a museum. Greenway's simpler though nonetheless stylish St. James' Church, Sydney's oldest, is close-by on King Street.

29

Retracing one's steps northeastwards along Art Gallery Road into the green heart of the Domain, one approaches the Art Gallery of New South Wales. Established in 1874, this stately building designed by the Colonial Architect W. L. Vernon was extended in 1988 to accommodate its wide collection of Australian, Asian, and European art. The Yiribana Gallery, the world's largest collection of work by Aboriginal and Torres Strait Islander artists, opened in 1994.

The rolling parkland of the Domain, developed as Governor Macquarie's private garden (or domain) extends all the way north to the glistening waters of Farm Cove. Today the expansive lawns enjoy a more democratic life with outdoor concerts in summer and Sunday soap-box preachers, come rain or shine. In their central section lie the Royal Botanical Gardens, home to a luxurious variety of indigenous and foreign plant-life, from tropical species growing gargantuan beneath the glass-house pyramid to the miniature rows of aromatic, culinary and medicinal herbs in the Herb Garden.

31

30

29. View of Sydney from the Domain
30. Botanical Gardens
31. Hyde Park Barracks
32. Il Porcellino – bronze sculpture of a wild boar in front of the Sydney hospital (close to the Botanic Garden). Touching its snout is supposed to bring good luck – this belief is practised a lot as you can see by its gold-shimmering nose

At the edge of the Botanical Gardens stands Greenway's striking early Gothic Revival building, home to the Sydney Conservatorium of Music. Originally designed as stables and servants' quarters for Government House, "Greenway's folly" was considered too costly for its purpose. Indeed, the architect never recouped the monies he himself invested in it, and died penniless as a result!

At the very tip of the Domain is the stone bench carved into the rock where Elizabeth Macquarie, the Governor's wife, would pause in her daily constitutional to delight in the exhaustive views across the harbour. After an afternoon spent traipsing through the Domain, even the rock-hewn Mrs Macquarie's Chair seems rather relaxing, especially in the twilight hours as the sun sets over the Opera House and Sydney Harbour Bridge.

Chinatown and Darling Harbour

Chinatown and Darling Harbour, the paired neighbourhoods which cohabit the area that cups the city centre to the west and south, are an urban odd couple. Chinatown which dates from the 1850s is chaotic and cluttered, whilst Darling Harbour, Australia's largest urban redevelopment project designed to coincide with the bicentennial celebrations of 1988, is sparse and ordered. Though vibrant by day, much of Chinatown's activity is indoors and nocturnal. Darling Harbour on the other hand, serves as an outdoor leisure park whose many attractions are deserted by night. Together they function as an organic whole, like the precisely choreographed natural environment of the Chinese Gardens which run along their common border. A gift from Sydney's sister city Guandong, this exotic collocation of pavilions, lakes and greenery offers a tranquil respite from the turmoil of tourism and business which encroach upon it from both sides.

33. The Chinese Gardens, the green seam that joins Chinatown to Darling Harbour, were designed according to gardening principles that date back to the 5th century.
34. Sydney Opera House and Harbour Bridge. The Sydney Opera House took fourteen troubled years to build. When actual costs exceeded those anticipated, the shortfall was met by lotteries. The original design by Joern Utzon was modified and he left halfway through the project, never to see it completed.
35. Chinatown at night

34

Chinatown owes its origins to the influx of Chinese immigrants during the gold rushes of the mid-nineteenth century. Historically centred around Dixon and Hay Streets at the edge of the city's produce markets, Chinatown has risen and fallen to the rhythms of commercial tides and immigrant waves. Today it has expanded to encompass the Haymarket area, its population similarly extending to immigrants from all over South-East Asia, Japan and Hong Kong. Its streets are a frenetic cluster of herbalists and hand-made noodle shops, Shanghai dumpling diners and cavernous Hong Kong style

36

37

36. Crossing-keeper's hut on the Pyrmont bridge (swing-bridge) in Darling Harbour
37. Sydney's monorail was the source of great controversy at the time it was built. A ride on the "monster rail" offers great views of the harbour and some of the city's building sites.

yum cha halls. There are Chinese-language cinemas, covert gaming parlours, and arcades jammed with bargain jewellery and clothing. Paddy's Market, Sydney's largest covered bazaar which has occupied five different sites in the neighbourhood since first opening, continues to attract weekend crowds to its brimming stalls. The Capitol Theatre, a splendidly restored 1920s movie palace lures those too tired to shop or eat, into its Florentine Garden interior with lavish musical productions. What better place to see a performance of *Miss Saigon*?

38

38, 39, 40. Details of the Sydney Opera House
41. Opera House and tall ship in harbour
42. Sydney Harbour

39

40

In the early days of British settlement, Darling Harbour or Cockle Bay as it was then known (it was renamed in honour of the seventh governor of New South Wales, Ralph Darling) was an industrial workplace and international maritime centre. Throughout the first half of the nineteenth century, the waterfront was clotted with working-class cottages, bawdy houses and thieves' dens. Railroad yards flanked the docks from which a local trade in coal, wool and other merchandise were shipped for export. By the late twentieth century, it is tempting to say, the area had become a shell of its former self. With the decline in commercial activity (due to the advent of container shipping) the waterfront deteriorated into a congested wasteland of abandoned wharves and warehouses. In the 1980s the shorefront was reclaimed and transformed into a huge pedestrian mall flecked with Philip Cox's nautical themed architecture and loftily threaded by a monorail link to the city centre. Today it proffers all the trappings of recreational tourism, from the Harbourside Festival Marketplace (a monster-sized shopping mall) to the Panasonic IMAX theatre and the Sydney Aquarium. Designed by Percy Allen, The Pyrmont Bridge which opened in 1902 links Darling Harbour to Pyrmont. A walk over this, the world's oldest electrically operated swingspan

43

43. Tidal Cascades, designed by
    Robert Woodward (who also designed the
    El Alamein fountain in Kings Cross)
44. Pavillion in the grounds of the
    Chinese Gardens

45

46

45. Darling Harbour with monorail
46. View from the Centre Point on the monorail
47. A warship

bridge, is well-rewarded with some of the most spectacular views of the western cityscape, whose glass and steel skyscrapers dazzlingly reflect the sunny harbour waters. Pyrmont, once a concentration of quarries, refineries and warehouses was an integral part of Sydney's nineteenth-century waterfront industry, and despite the glaring twentieth-century backdrop, a sense of Sydney Harbour's maritime past can be recaptured here aboard one of the historic ships moored in the National Maritime Museum. You can be transported to yet another age in a jaunt through the Harris Street Motor Museum, a quirky collection of vehicles that celebrates a century of automotive history.

48. Sydney Harbour Bridge
49. Sydney Fish Markets, second only in the world perhaps to
    Tokyo's Tsujiki, offer the freshest of Australia's exquisite seafood.
50. Sculpture with the symbol of Olympiad 2000 in front of the
    Convention Hall

48

49

50

With pit-stops at the Sydney Convention and Exhibition Centre and Star City, Sydney's one casino, a saunter southwards leads to Ultimo whose Powerhouse Museum, housed in a converted old power station, is one of Sydney's most cutting-edge exhibition sites. If the lonely streets of Ultimo, seem like a dead end, a short trail to the shores of Blackwattle Bay to the west, finds you awash in the crowded sea of vendors at the Sydney Fish Markets.

52

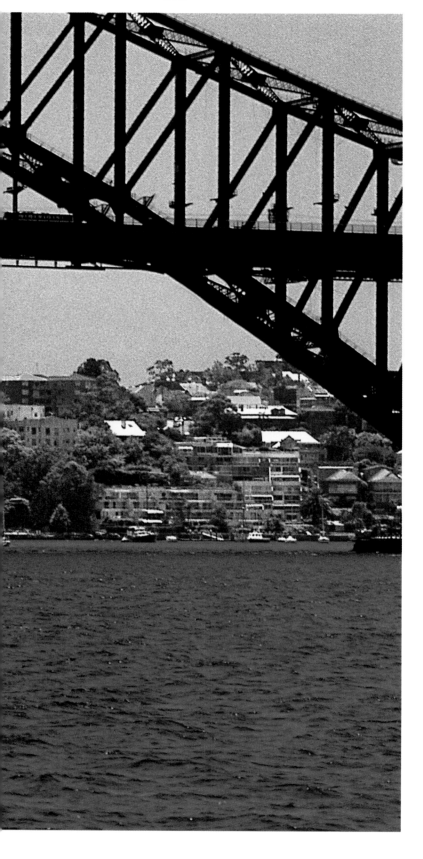

53

51. Darling Harbour
52. Sydney Harbour Bridge
53. Aerial view of Sydney Harbour

The Rocks and Circular Quay

After declaring Botany Bay unfit for settlement, Captain Arthur Phillip and his motley crew of rum-soaked seamen, convicts and guards sailed on to Sydney Cove. On January 26, 1788 under a barrage of spears and stones launched by the local aboriginals, the officers of the First Fleet pitched their tents on the eastern section of the quay while in the rocky outcrop to the west, their raucous human cargo was deposited. Over the next few years, this makeshift collection of convict and military dwellings was transformed into a maritime hub with the waterfront a tangled belt of bond-stores and warehouses, grog shops and brothels. In this Dickensian maze of cobble-stoned alleys lined with open sewers, whalers and ticket-of-leavers, smugglers, convicts, soldiers and prostitutes jostled each other in what had become Australia's most densely populated urban community. While the *nouveaux riches* built terrace homes in the hills during the 1820s and 1830s, in the slums below, razor gangs with names like "the Cabbage-Tree Boys", "the Golden Dragons" and the "Forty Thieves" terrorized the local populace. As time wore on, the port area grew even more squalid and in 1900 a wave of bubonic plague broke over the turbulent shore and whole areas had to be razed. A decline in commercial activity, due to the displacement of shipping and storage facilities away from Circular Quay conspired to empty the district even further. By the 1920s the neighbourhood was in such disrepair that no-one resisted the demolition of entire rows of Victorian houses to clear space for the construction of the Sydney Harbour Bridge.

54. The Rocks Square
55. Sydney's oldest watering-hole, the *Hero of Waterloo*, in the Rocks
56. The Concert Hall in the Sydney Opera House, the building's largest auditorium, seats 2,690 people.

57. The Rocks
58. Stairs at The Argyle Cut. In 1843, hundred of convicts began carving through the solid sandstone with hammer and chisel to create a roadway joining Sydney Cove to Darling Harbour in the west. It took eighteen years and extra government labour to complete.
59. Wooden door at Cadman's Cottage

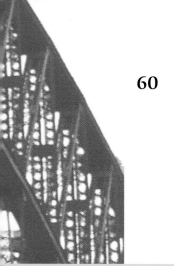

60

Today under the shadow of world's largest single-span bridge, (whose nicknames include the "Coat Hanger," the "Toast Rack" and the "Iron Lung"), the Rocks have been reborn. Due to the preservation efforts of 1970s activists, a plan to level the area was abandoned and many of the old Georgian and Victorian structures were restored, their bluestone façades buffed and polished and padded with koala soft toys. Like Boston's Fanueil Hall district, this historic precinct is now a tourist centre with convict-era storehouses such as The Argyle Centre and Campbell's Storehouses recast as boutique shopping galleries and many sites, like The Sailors' Home, the Merchants' House and Cadman's Cottage (Sydney's oldest building) preserved as museums. After a pint or two at Sydney's oldest pub, the *Hero of Waterloo*, it is not difficult to picture the wild Hogarthian tableau of convicts, sailors and women of ill-repute rough-housing through the oldest of Sydney's waterfront back-streets!

61

60. Sydney Harbour Bridge
61. Wrought-iron ornaments at the Rocks
62. Sydney Opera House
63. The Rocks
64. The Wharf Theatre on Walsh Bay is home to the Sydney Theatre Company.

62

GOLDFIELDS

Adjacent to the Rocks is Circular Quay, the main commuter terminal for ferries, jet-cats and water taxis that shuttle passengers to a variety of harbour destinations. Rush-hour travellers sailing home and leisurely sight-seers en route to some of the north shore tourist attractions cannot but help take a moment on deck to inhale the harbour tang and embrace the theatrical city views.

To the western side of the Quay, in the former Maritime Services Board building, a six-storey mock art deco building of the 1950s is the Museum of Contemporary Art. Yet for one of the most famous moments in contemporary art, it is only a short walk along the spectacular Eastern Promenade to what Robert Hughes has called, "the biggest environmental site-specific sculpture south of the Equator": The Sydney Opera House. Sharing equal billing with the Sydney Harbour Bridge on the opposite end of the curving quay, Sydney's Opera House, designed by Danish archictect Joern Utzon, is the city's foremost architectural icon. Beneath its billowing white ceramic-tiled sails, five theatres – a concert hall, an opera theatre, a drama theatre, a cinema and recording hall – and two restaurants offer their siren call to culture vultures from near and far.

68

65. Façades – Circular Quay
66. Detail of the Sydney Opera House
67. The Wharfs
68. View of the Opera House from the sea
69. St. Mary's Cathedral

Darlinghurst and Surry Hills

While Kings Cross is noticeably devoid of royalty, the adjacent neighbourhoods of Darlinghurst and Surry Hills are a densely populated cosmopolitan enclave of queens and fairy princesses. Darlinghurst, otherwise known is the gay ghetto, is the epicentre of gay life in the Southern hemisphere where towering coifs are sustained by so much hair-spray that they poke through the infamous hole in Sydney's ozone layer. The main drag is Oxford Street, which sashays all the way from Hyde Park through Surry Hills to Paddington and beyond. Along this seemingly endless commercial artery, the local glitterati dazzle on a stage set with an unremitting succession of ultra-cool clothing shops, packed cafés, pubs, motels, transvestite cabarets, hair-salons and night-clubs.

Up Crown Street, which dissects the lower end of Oxford Street is Surry Hills, a tumbledown terrain of low-rent terraces and tiny lanes filled with huge potted plants. As yet ungentrified, there is much adventure in its many ethnic restaurants, theatres and the Brett Whitely Studio, a gallery housing the work of Australia's beloved tragic-genius artist. Back on Oxford Street, the pulsing dance-beat crescendoes midway up the thoroughfare in Taylor Square (party headquarters), then diverts into an exotic medley of Balkan, Thai and Indian restaurants and finally tapers off into the more heady rhythms of art-house cinemas and all-night bookstores abutting Paddington. Darlinghurst Gaol built in 1841 and converted in 1921 into the East Sydney College of the Arts (today it is the Sydney Institute of Technology) marks the point where Darlinghurst descends into Kings Cross and is a daunting symbol of Sydney's penal past.

Every year in February, Sydney is besotted with the Gay and Lesbian festival. For an entire month, Sydney's arguably most dominant culture is celebrated in musical events, street performances, film, live theatre and the visual arts. The cultural extravaganza culminates in the orgiastic Mardi Gras parade down Oxford Street in March under the mayor's benevolent gaze and the frowns of fundamentalist hecklers praying for rain. Three quarters of a million local and overseas spectators line the pavement to ogle at the nocturnal sea of floats, feathers, leather, latex and sequins, dykes on bikes and macho musclemen. This spectacular swirling human tide ultimately spills into the Royal agricultural show-grounds where a mammoth dance party rages ecstatically into the dying night.

70. Also a part of history:
    Islay, the dog of Queen Victoria
71. A Mardi Gras mermaid
72. Elizabeth Bay

Kings Cross

On the eastern fringes of the city, land-locked between the upmarket *arrondissement* of Potts Point to the north, and the gay mecca of Darlinghurst to the south, lies Kings Cross – Sydney's most notorious neighbourhood. Originally named Queens Cross (for Queen Victoria) until King Edward became its namesake, Kings Cross is anything but a regal domain. With its all-night bars, night-clubs, prostitutes, drug dealers, strip joints and 24-hour XXX theatres, "The Cross", as it is affectionately known to Sydneysiders is the pilgrimage point to which all varieties of sinners flock. Sometimes dangerous and always lurid, its neon lights flashing temptation throughout the day and night, Kings Cross has historically been Sydney's centre for what lies on the edge.

In the 1920s, Kings Cross – Sydney's then equivalent to Chicago's South Side – was riddled with rival mobs battling it out. As the gunfire of the gangsters died down, in the 1930s the Cross retired unquietly into a new life as a bohemian haven. Here settled fringe-dwellers of all stripes (no longer the regulation black and white!), including scores of avant-garde poets and artists. Another sea-change occurred in the neighbourhood in the forties, when U.S. Sailors headed to the district in pursuit of R and R (Rest and Recreation). The World War II period not only saw the blossoming of the ill-repute of Kings Cross but also, with the influx of European refugees, its reputation for ethnic diversity.

Kings Cross began its official reign as the vice capital of Australia in the 1960s. During the Vietnam era, American G.I.s once again descended, pockets full of cash and hearts full of unholy desires. Many locals attribute the dilution of the neighbourhood's charm within a sea of crass commercialism to this period. Yet in the midst of the tacky signs and sometimes unsavoury hyperactivity, charming pockets remain intact. Tree-lined side streets that snake off the main trashy strip of Darlinghurst Road are graced with terrace homes and glamorous boutique hotels. Cafés serving up *foccacia* and *caffè lattes* are filled with inner-city hipsters glancing up from manuscripts to watch the passing spectacle in all its multiformity.

73. A crow fighting with a plastic bag.
74. The El Alamein fountain (1961) by architects Woodward and Taranto
75. Graffitti recalling the art work of the Aborigines

Indeed the Cross is a fusion cuisine – sometimes delicious, sometimes unappetizing – of a panoply of ingredients that appeal to all palates. Luxury apartment blocks sidle up to backpacker hostels, international hotels nestle in between peep-show booths, classy restaurants of international fame jostle with brothels, massage parlors front up to road-side Chinese acupressure stalls. The Cross is the confluence of the good-life and low-life, of populations transient and local (and local transients!). Even the landmarks of the Cross reflect the amiable polarity of the quarter: the capricious El Alamein fountain in the Fitzroy Gardens (to whose dysfunctional rhythms passers-by intone "She loves me, she loves me not") to the monumental *Coca Cola* sign that hovers over William Street, inextinguishable.

Paddington

"Paddo", as it is known to Aussies with their love of abbreviation, is one of Sydney's most *recherché* neighbourhoods. A "village in the city," Paddington preens itself like a giant glossy-coated cat only four kilometres from the city centre. Stretching from the Victoria Barracks in the west along Oxford Street to Centennial Park, the neighbourhood radiates outwards in an ambiguous jumble of elegant lanes towards Woolhara. Its beautifully restored terrace homes with their iron lace balconies and gates, Grecian-style friezes, cornices and parapets, urns, serpents and other imaginative plaster motifs are justly celebrated. Representing some of the most to-die-for properties around, Paddington's terraces have provoked a veritable real-estate fray amongst city professionals and arty entrepreneurs!

76, 77. Paddington properties

77

Named after the London borough, Paddington is not however just a stoically preserved architectural museum. This beloved suburb also vaunts a vivacious street-culture which bursts alive on Saturdays when the Paddington Village bazaar opens its serendipitous gates to bargain-hunters and exotica-scavengers. Other times during the week, the pace slackens and a leisurely stroll uncovers a myriad of speciality shops. Antique dealers and trendy art galleries, innovative and expensive designer clothing shops, bookstores, stylish cafés, interior design studios, quaint pubs and up-scale restaurants uncoil along Paddo's stretch of Oxford Street and dot the narrow, leafy lanes sloping down from it towards the harbour. The green expanses and groves of eucalyptus and paperbarks in Centennial Park also offer their allure to promenades on foot, bicycle and horseback. Picnickers and amateur Monets alike, are always to be found enjoying this historical common.

The original Paddington was developed in the 1830s as a week-end getaway for the Georgian gentry. This period of glory was short-lived – immense mansions were demolished and the properties were subdivided. However, a number of these palatial five- or six-storey homes still grace the steep north-eastern streets of Five Ways and Glenmore Road. The famed Victorian terraces of Paddington were built in the 1840s and 1850s. With the construction of the Victoria Barracks, Paddington became a housing community for the site's quarrymen, carpenters and other artisans. Clusters of stone houses, some of which still remain, along with tightly packed terrace houses sprung up in rapid succession. Once the soldiers, the artisans and their families had settled in, shopkeepers and publicans quickly followed suit. Development declined by the 1900s when it became fashionable to flee the city and replant soiled roots in the emerging "garden" suburbs further afield. After WWII, following a second stampede towards the outer suburbs, the neighbourhood fell into complete ruin.

78. A typical wrought-iron balcony in Paddington
79. Pastel shades of a Paddington terrace home
80. House in Paddington

80

Paddington's renaissance dates from the 1960s. The swinging tide of residential fashion sent waves of urbanites in search of decorative inner-city abodes into the suburb. Gradually, then exponentially, the process of gentrification burgeoned. From its modest working-class origins, and fallow slum era, Paddo has become an exemplary model of unplanned urban restoration and the *ne plus ultra* of chic.

82

83

81. Paddington Property
82. The "Lord Nelson"
83. *London Tavern* sign

Beyond Sydney

Nestling beneath the rugged cliffs which line the city's eastern shore is a site sacred to Sydneysiders, a hallowed national institution and a scene as famous to foreigners as the iconic Opera House and Sydney Harbour Bridge. Welcome to Bondi Beach! The golden surf-swept sands of Bondi (which means "the sound of waves breaking over rocks") are inundated summer long with the dreamy drone of sun worshipping hordes stretched out on a carpet of towels extending from the quaint Bondi Pavilion (of 1928) down to the wavy waters. All the archetypal images of Australian culture are here, from the muscular sun-bronzed life-savers to the bleached-haired surfies that tackle the famous foamy crests from dawn to dusk and the Bondi Iceberg club swimmers who brave the windy sea all year round. Over recent years, the sea-side community has seen a blossoming of chic cafés built along its main waterfront promenade, Campbell Parade, but the neighbourhood's charm has always been in its rough and tumble, laid-back, atmosphere.

84. Hamilton Lund
85. One-man sailing regatta
86. The sun and surf of Bondi Beach

The breathtaking walk southwards along the cliffs from Bondi down the coast via Tamarama (or "Glamorama" as the locals call it), Bronte and Clovelly beaches to Coogee Beach is one of the truly ecstatic pleasures that this hedonistic city holds. Further south and following the coastline as it curves inwards towards the west, one lands at the historic Botany Bay, the place where Captain Cook and the crew of the *Endeavour* first set foot on 'Terra Australis' on April 29, 1770. Following the coastline north of Bondi and looping round towards the city centre, lie some of Sydney's most picturesque waterfront suburbs. Set along the shorefronts of the bays whose names they bear, Watson's Bay, Rose Bay, Double Bay (or "Double Pay" as the Sydneysiders refer to it) and Elizabeth Bay, these exclusive residential neighbourhoods with their dazzling views are the stuff that Sydneysiders' dreams are made of. The site of dreams unfulfilled (Sydney's notorious suicide spot) is the bite in the cliffs around Watson's Bay known as "the Gap".

87. Beach
88. Aerial view of Homebush Bay, the site of the Olympic Games
89. The 2000 Olympics pool

87

90

90. Sydney has a lot of beautiful beaches to offer.
91. Manly Beach (also known as "God's own country") was named by Captain Arthur Phillip for the "confidence and manly behaviour" of the local Aboriginals. The beachfront is lined by tall Norfolk Island planted when the area was developed as a posh vacation resort for Sydneysiders. "Seven miles from Sydney and a thousand miles from care."
92. Sailing regatta

91

In many ways, the North shore of Sydney is a mirror image of the Sydney across the harbour. It has a central business district, North Sydney, which has grown-up as a spill-over from the confined area of the official CBD; elegant residential neighbourhoods, located mostly on the Upper North shore; delightful parkland areas, such as Lane Cove National Park; historical enclaves like the stone cottages of Hunter's Hill, and Victorian buildings such as Admiralty House and the rambling Gothic harbourside residence of

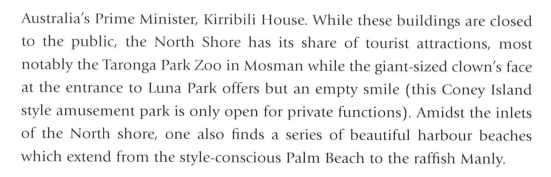

94

Australia's Prime Minister, Kirribili House. While these buildings are closed to the public, the North Shore has its share of tourist attractions, most notably the Taronga Park Zoo in Mosman while the giant-sized clown's face at the entrance to Luna Park offers but an empty smile (this Coney Island style amusement park is only open for private functions). Amidst the inlets of the North shore, one also finds a series of beautiful harbour beaches which extend from the style-conscious Palm Beach to the raffish Manly.

Manly, located on an isthmus just north of North Head, is Sydney's most renowned beach after Bondi. In fact it is two beaches, the secluded harbour-side Manly Cove and the ever-popular ocean surfing beach. No longer the exclusive vacation resort it was at the turn of the twentieth century, tourist-friendly Manly still remains one of Sydney's most alluring sandy pockets.

93. Site of the Olympic Games
94. Stand detail of the stadium Australia
95. With full sails

Publishing Director: Jean-Paul Manzo

Text: Yvonne Shafir

Design and layout: : Newton Harris Design Partnership

Cover and jacket : Cédric Pontes

Publishing assistants: Paula von Chmara, Aurélia Hardy

Photograph credits:

Klaus H. Carl : 10, 15, 17, 19, 21, 22, 24, 31, 32, 34, 36, 38, 39, 10, 42, 43b, 45, 47, 48, 50, 52, 59, 60, 61, 62, 65, 66, 67, 68, 69, 70, 72, 73, 75, 80, 82, 83, 85, 87, 90, 92, 93, 94, 95.

Australian Tourist Commission : 1, 2, 5, 6, 7, 11, 12, 13, 14, 16, 25, 26, 27, 30, 33, 35, 37, 41, 44, 49, 51, 53, 54, 55, 56, 57, 58, 64, 71, 74, 77, 79, 81, 84, 88, 89, 91

Sigrid Wolf-Feix : 4, 8, 19, 23, 46, 77, 78

Monika Mager: 9, 20, 29, 43, 63

Parkstone Press Ltd
Printed and bound in Singapore
ISBN 1 85995 730 7

© Parkstone Press, London, England, 2000